The Waiting Room

poems by

Christine Strevinsky

Finishing Line Press
Georgetown, Kentucky

The Waiting Room

ACKNOWLEDGMENTS

"Moving Day" appeared previously in *U.S. 1 Worksheets*,
"The Widows" in the *Louisiana Journal of College Writing*

Many thanks are due to the members of the Green River Writers for their
patience and their critical input to these poems; particular thanks are due to
Mary E. O'Dell and E. Gail Chandler without whose technical knowhow this
manuscript would still be foundering in computer neverland, and who deserves
many kudos for her expertise. Thanks are also due to Andrea Gereighty, the
founder of the New Orleans Poetry Forum wherever her soul may be these days..

Thanks are also due to my son Mitchell Strevinsky and daughter-in-law Laura for
putting up with me and my endless avalanche of books.

Publisher: Leah Maines

Editor: Christen Kincaid

Cover Art: E. Gail Chandler

Author Photo: E. Gail Chandler

Cover Design: Elizabeth Maines

Printed in the USA on acid-free paper.
Order online: www.finishinglinepress.com
            also available on amazon.com

Author inquiries and mail orders:
Finishing Line Press
P. O. Box 1626
Georgetown, Kentucky 40324
U. S. A.

Table of Contents

for Tosiek and Benji

neither of whom got to be old

Five Women Riding the Wheels Bus to a Podiatric Appointment

Joy climbs on unaided, stops, gazes at
the eleven unoccupied seats, fiddles with a button
Where should I sit? She tries the first row. Gets up.
Goes to the rear. Up again. Stops next to Sue
already in one of the middle seats. Makes a motion
as if to climb over Sue's feet. Sue sets her oxygen down.
Joy moves again, sits in front, first at the window
then back on the aisle. Fumbles with the seat belt
until the driver snaps the buckle in.

Linda waits for the lift to come down.
Her walker is laden with bags and a box of Krispy Kremes.
No time for breakfast. Planted solidly behind Sue
she taps a shoulder. *Wanna donut? Your daughter home yet?*

Ella Mae hugs the driver before mounting the lift.
How's ever'body? Hello, sugar. Sure's nasty out.
She yanks the belt out to full length, snaps it in.
She rearranges her cape, yanks her hat lower,
roots in a pocket, comes up with a cough drop.

Dodie gets on with the driver's assistance.
Ella Mae has told Sue Dodie won't use the lift—
too proud for that—and lies about her age.
Sue rolls her eyes at Ella Mae; they smirk at each other.

They groan in a chorus when the bus hits a bump.
When they gonna fix them potholes? Nobody answers.
Everybody shrugs. *Hope Doc Whatsis—can't remember
that long name—don't run late like last time, but them toenails
is killin' me, and I can't do them myself no more.*
A chorus of *Me neithers* erupts just as the bus stops.
They gather their belongings and with *Ouch, Oof*
and *Lord, have mercy* they stand up to move to the exits.

J. B. Vadell—Accountant, Retired

He's out early
before the sun rises
to walk his beagle/poodle mix
his late wife loved
more than a child;
he lights his first Marlboro
pausing under the still lit lamp-post
while Coco squats
beside the oak.

He waits patiently
as she sniffs at
an interesting drainpipe,
picks up the paper
from the doormat
and heads for the kitchen
to pour the first cup
from Mr. Coffee
brewed while he
and Coco were out.

He watches
the six o'clock news
eating his daily bowl of grits
while Coco gnaws kibble,
thinks he must
do the laundry soon.

Neighbors

They have lived in adjoining trailers for years;
Jack, on the left, resembles a pair of calipers—
all elbows and knee angles. A cigarette dangles
perpetually from the corner of his lips;
he coughs, sunken chest heaving.

Walter, in the right-hand trailer, is fat
with triple chins and an enormous belly
encased in 5X pants; when he bends over,
he treats the world to a view of his hairy crack.
He owns a red Chevy truck and refuses
to let Jack ride in it.

I don't wanna my truck to stink like no tobacco
he says by way of explanation, but will,
albeit grudgingly, bring Jack the odd loaf of bread
or a gallon of milk. He refuses to buy him cigarettes.

They both ride the same small bus to the senior center
Monday through Friday, but do not sit together.
Walter sits up front spread over the double seat,
Jack on the long bench all the way at the rear of the bus.

En Route to the Senior Center

We pass two graveyards.
The smaller one, with graves
scattered randomly
over a piece of flat ground
holds only a scant dozen
or so of headstones;
an aged trailer lists along one side
its concrete apron littered
with lawnmower carcasses and
dismembered bicycles.
A yellow dog of mixed parentage
with mangy fur guards its door.

The second burial ground
with headstones ranged like teeth
in uneven rows contains, perhaps,
as many as three dozen graves
perching on an uneven hillside.
On most mornings, two goats and a donkey
are tethered to stakes driven between
the flattened mounds.
A remnant of a barn, all gray weathered wood
clings to the hillside above them.

The goats watch us with knowing eyes as we pass.

Miz Eula Mae's Birthday

T'weren't but two years we was married,
Hiram and me. We was both sixteen in 1915
when we got hitched and Hiram went to France.
I never knowed where he lay, all they tol' me is France.
I lost my one boy in '44, in the Pacific, the ocean?
He done never come home.

Alfie, what was my second husband
he got liver trouble. Doctor said t'was
on account Alfie was a drinking man.
So I was a widder woman again with four girls.
Only one a them is livin' today.

Seem like ever'body is dead 'cept me
and my one girl and her one boy.
They's coming today cause it's my birthday
and the folks here, in the home,
is giving me a big party.

You should a heard the whooping and hollering
when the mailman done come
and brung me the letter from the president hisself,
from the Whitehouse wishing me a happy birthday.
And Miz Thelma says you is here so's I can be on teevee.
I guess folks is curious to see somebody
what's as old as I am.

I guess I should thank the good Lord
I can still see pretty good now the doctor
took them catracks offen my eyes
and I can still hear with no hearing aids.
But I can't walk no more and things don't
taste good no more like my taster done died.

Hunnert three is a long time to be living
special when almost all your kin is gone,
but I guess being alive is better than being dead.
Life ain't all bad, even when you is as old as me.

Patriarch

My granduncle Adam
married his fourth wife
in his hundred second year.
He'd buried the other three
and joked he robbed the cradle—
wife number four was
only sixty-six.

He still kept the garden;
grew rhubarb, red currants,
parsnips, gooseberries and roses.
Claimed his hens laid
the best and biggest eggs.

He got up with sun,
went to bed when it did
except on Sundays and holy days
including Corpus Christi
when he carried the standard
in the procession.

He had his own teeth;
gave credit to hard black bread
and all the roots he ate
(rutabagas in particular)
And the salt he rubbed daily
Into his gums.

He died at a hundred and seven—
did not go gently into that good night
but rode his horse full speed
to meet the reaper.
Hooves sheared his skull
as his steed fell
in April's last snow.

Old Mr. Henry

He plants a garden every spring
measuring off rows with lengths of string
rooted out of the kitchen junk drawer.
Radishes, turnips, lettuce, fronds of dill
for the cucumbers he puts in the back
by the fence.

He refurbishes the scarecrow
in his own clothes, deliberating
ever so slowly whether to give up
the red plaid shirt or the blue paisley
with the Nehru collar.

He sits on the oak stump
sorting seeds (he never buys any)
he has saved in old envelopes
calculating how much ground
he'll need this year.

Sometimes he plants at night
(he believes in *Farmer's Almanac*
which says root crops should go in
by the dark of the moon)
and drives his wife crazy
coming to bed with ice cold feet
long past midnight.

On sunny days he sits outside
eyes closed, face turned to the sky.
He says he can hear the plants grow.
He talk to them, but seldom to his wife,
in the same indulgent tone he used
talking to his children when they were small.

He believes nothing's as good as what he grows.

Old Lady Eckles

lives at the end of a one lane
steep gravel road
in a gray house
surrounded by trees
choked by kudzu vines.
From the small clearing
which encircles it
she cannot see her neighbors—
the Burdocks—
even though they live
a scant quarter of a mile away.

She shares her dwelling
with a medley of cats
most as gray as the house
although there is the odd calico
among them as well as a tabby.
There is also a lone dog
part collie by the looks of it.

Each spring she plants
a garden beside the house—
a few tomato vines, bush beans
a cucumber or two
squash and some melons.

Out front there's a flower bed
with irises, lilies and marigolds.
She likes to pluck a few buds
to put into the small vase
in front of the pictures
of her dead husbands.

Daily

She says good morning
before getting out of bed,
pats the urn's dome fondly
and pads to the bathroom.

In between brushing her teeth,
showering and dressing
she fills him in on her day's agenda.

Over coffee and toast
she relates the latest gossip
she'd picked up at the store.

Today, there's the thing about Buddy
You know she tells him
how bad he got—
wouldn't eat, couldn't walk no more.

The vet said Buddy was
ninety-nine in dog years.
I had to let him go.

But I guess you know it already.
Buddy must've found you by now.
Least, I hope so.

I think dogs go
to the same heaven people do.
It stands to reason,
            don't it?

Agnes Has Her Say
(1883-1949)

I was one of three sisters, the one with the limp.
The one who sewed dance gowns for Mae and Lil
but never got asked to go; never had a single beau.
The one relegated to the attic, the maid's quarters.

I got shunted between my sisters' houses
after Ma and Pa died and became the house maid,
cook, and nanny to my nieces and nephews
to earn my keep and roof.

When we got old I went to live with Francie,
Mae's oldest, in much the same capacity;
never got asked to the parties even though
I baked the cakes and polished the silver.

I kept to myself. Not that anyone cared,
but, at least, Francie let me keep a cat.
She did say to keep him in my room,
not let him roam the house. He was lame, like me.

I ate my meals in the kitchen, or my room
with Purkin for company. I made catnip mice
for his birthday; nobody remembered mine.
For Christmas, I made a little tree out of their trimmings.

Purkin died the day before I did.
I think he knew I was ready to go.
No one missed him. Only the house missed me
until someone realized Agnes no longer did the work.

From the Back of Aunt Lucy's Closet

She kept letters
from people long dead
hidden in a wooden box
whose carved lid
bore images
of velvety flowers
that grow only
on the rocky outcrops
of the Tatra mountains.

The yellowed pages
crumble under careless
fingers; the ink has paled,
but the small squares affixed
to the corners of the envelopes
still glow.

The blue ribbon that
binds the pages
of a separate bundle
disintegrates when untied;
the signatures
on these letters
are all the same

             Twój zawsze
                Antek

             Yours always
                Tony

To her grandson
only the stamps matter.

Moving Day

In the Sheltering Palms Village's
brand new condo the walls
are too vanilla bland
for posters of Baez and Joplin;
Timothy Leary's portrait
clipped from *Newsweek*
won't fit in here either.

Did you really wear these?
They consign the bellbottoms
and the pink hot pants
to the Goodwill box.
My cast iron skillet joins them—
Got you some nice Teflon ones—
as do my old aluminum pots.

One small U-Haul will suffice
to transport the rest to the new pad.
I've tucked my old eight-tracks
between sheets and towels.
My copy of *Howl* cringes
underneath my underwear.

House on the Corner Lot

The kids avoid it
even in daytime;
believe in their small hearts
something monstrous
lives there.

Behind the windows
obscured by rampant hedges
a figure moves,
pulls aside the gray curtains
peers at the outside.

Sometimes at night
thin music drifts out
from behind the shut door,
winds its way down the street
sending shivers
down listeners spines.

The mailman seldom stops
at the curbside box;
leaves only circulars,
government envelopes,
shopping catalogs
no one sees retrieved.

The groceries brought
by a man in a dun car,
the rare packages
left by the front door
are pulled inside
by a sweater-covered arm.

At night, a lone glimmer shows
above the hedge tops.

Uncle Howard

His checkbook mocks him.
Numbers gnaw at his pen
and someone has moved
his favorite hardware store.

His furnace whispers
malicious gossip while the fridge
complains about the boots
left in the veggie crisper.

He swears his house hides
on the wrong street so that
he has to circle the neighborhood
to find it each time he leaves it.

He says a headless girl lives
in his hallway closet
among the old umbrellas,
mackintoshes and shoes.

His mouth trembles when
he nicks his chin shaving
or when he mistakes
Preparation H for toothpaste.

He tells me Howie Junior
forgot to call on his birthday.
I haven't the heart to tell him
Howie died in 'Nam years ago.

Fred and Edie's House

smells sour like a dishrag
left in the sink too long;
other evil odors assail the nose
of the unwary visitor—
stale urine leaches out
of the upholstery,
mingles with last week's
tuna fish casserole.

Martha makes duty calls
to her in-laws even though
Freddie Junior has been dead
for more than five years.
She makes sure there's food
but no longer takes Edie shopping,
not since the day Edie pelted
the cashier with kiwis and smacked
the Piggly-Wiggly manager
with a link of Polish sausage.

She has been putting off
the inevitable bracing herself
for the scene Edie will no doubt create;
Fred will sit and mumble oblivious
to everything except the beer can,
the only thing he manages not to spill.

The woman from Social Services said
she'd be there at half past one.
All Martha has to do now is wait.

Ruthie

In memory of the Duck Lady of New Orleans

Her wheeled feet,
followed by webbed ones,
traverse the old Quarter streets.

She peers into strangers' faces
intent on finding someone
only she knows.

She depends on the kindness
of these strangers
for sustenance

amidst her ceaseless journeys
to destinations
no one else ever knows.

She is wise in the ways
of innocents and fools
who may also depend

on the kindness of strangers
and, like Ruthie, live lives
of endless wonder

somewhere between
the country of Nod and Neverland.

Crazy Rita

Rita yells at Jesus
who—she is sure of this—
lives behind the sheetrock
right above the headboard
 of her double bed.

She tells Him
He's falling down
on the job;
He hasn't gotten her
the promotion she deserves

and takes a claw hammer
to the wall. *Come outta there,
right now, Jesus* and shoves her arm
into the hole. *I'm gonna yank
that beard of yours out,
by the roots. Hear me, Jesus?*

She ignores the neighbors
pounding on her door,
the muffled epithets hurled her way,
the threats to call the cops.
*My prayers ain't good enough?
What about them candles
I lit at Saint Benilde's? Huh?*

Her broken fingernails
scrape the wall, leave bloody streaks
*Goddamn , Jesus, I'm gonna
tell Your Daddy on You!*

Mama

lives confined by
her dresser, bed, chair
and ottoman; the trees,
the traffic beyond her window
terrify the child
she's become.

She had run her company
single-handed, was perceived as
tough, able, and fair.
Her competitors said she could
chew you up and spit you out.

She whimpers, *Someone's out there,*
cowers in the chair and weeps.
Distracted by a bowl of ice cream
and Oreos she smiles
forgets the monsters under the bed.

In the kitchen, her daughters
drink coffee, shuffle through brochures
and chart her future.

Homesick

I want to go home.
Her friend mutes the soap.
It's such a nice place
she murmurs recalling
the spilled soup, the soiled underwear
she reported to the daughter.
I want to go home mingles with
the dialogue of *The Young and the Restless.*

She hopes she can still
the quavering voice by saying
You can play bingo with the other ladies
and thinks she'd rather
turn on the gas or swallow pills
than go to Fairhaven.

She promises to come on Sunday
as she flips the channels.
She can still hear *I want to go home*
as she flips the phone shut.

Waiting Room

I page through the *Geographic,*
Popular Mechanics, Home & Garden.
See nothing.

Others sit
tap fingers on purses,
swing feet,
avoid each other's eyes
half smiles congealed
on frozen faces.

Eyes lift
as a door opens;
scrubs emerge into sight
disappear again
having summoned
Mrs. Frangiss
Mr. Hubbler.

In the corner
a pothos sheds yellowed leaves.
Papers rustle.
A murmured *Thank you*
falls to the floor.

I sit.
Dread sits beside me.

An Ordinary Day

The old woman lay on concrete
under the midday July sun
her left leg bent at an odd angle,
catalogs and envelopes spread
in a corolla around her head.

A black cat with a white ascot
and socks meandered over,
touched his small nose to hers;
his whiskers brushed her lips.
She opened her eyes;
her mouth formed a word
but no sound issued forth.
The cat went off to do catly things.

The sun moved above
the silent street—no traffic
came through on this mid-week
ordinary working day—
the shadows lengthened.

A fly begun spelunking
in the old woman's nose—
another landed on the surface
of the opened unseeing eye.
The cat returned and sat nearby
licking the pads of his left paw.

A car pulled into the driveway next door.
A door slammed.

The Widows

In November, they visit the graves
bent on housekeeping tasks
of sweeping the leaves,
pulling weeds, discarding old wreaths.
They carry folded umbrellas
beneath their arms;
mums fill the jars they bring.

They brush aside brown foliage,
search out the rectangular outlines
covered by summer grass,
light new votive candles,
watch their flames flicker,
murmur *Pater Nosters* and *Ave Marias.*

They sit on cold stone benches
held by a reluctance
to leave for coffee shops,
movie houses and malls.

The cold travels upward to their chests;
they pull their coats tighter,
remain till daylight begins to dim
and leave, trailing Amens like beads.

Family Matriarch

A largish sepia photo
curled at the corners
marked on the back
in faded brown ink
May 18, 1825—January 11, 1918
Józefina Augustyniak.

It's the only known picture
of this woman who lies,
folded hands half hidden
by lace frills.
Her face, framed by a bonnet
tied with a ribbon bow
shows a firm mouth
and a strong chin.

Massive candles in tall holders
stand lit at the head
of her narrow coffin
whose cross-embossed lid
propped against the bier
faces the viewers.
But her portrait, affixed
to the coffin's foot
as dictated by custom
is invisible here.

Huddled in a tight group
behind the coffin
sit six women in black—
professional wailers whose open mouths
attest they are on the job—
a testament to her family's
love and devotion.

Family and Friends

They drift in singly
or in small groups,
clutch shredded tissues
in nervous hands,
smile damply at each other,
speak pleasantries
in lowered voices and
cast sideways glances
at the flower-banked coffin.

Body heat mingles
with the scent of gardenias,
the sharp tang of carnations
and the slightly singed odor
of spider mums arrayed
under the torchieres.

They merge in clusters
on tastefully gray sofas
along somber walls hung
with innocuous landscapes,
but avoid the stark folding chairs
ranged in neat rows
in the middle of the
Twilight Repose Room.

They kneel on prieux-dieus,
whisper *Hail Marys* and
Our Fathers as they bow their heads
over ruffled bosoms
and somber ties,
wield rosary beads between
pious folded hands and
pay homage to the waxy mannequin
in the satin-lined box.

In the back, in the Hospitality Room
with its coffee urn, donuts, and
bagels with cream cheese
their voices rise unrestrained
exchanging gossip about
that untimely baby, you-know-who's
fourth husband, and the drinking,
the tickets so-and-so has accumulated.
A bit later, led by a man in black,
they give dutiful replies with Amens
at each pause in the fulsome praises
and gratuitous prayers for the soul
of the recently departed.

Lastly, they accompany the coffin
on its journey to the hearse,
line up behind it for the procession
to its destination at the Garden of Memories.

In the Check-in Line

Never thought I'd be standing naked
waiting to be admitted
but it makes sense—
come in naked, go out naked.

Didn't expect it to be so mundane;
just like applying for a license—
long lines, harried clerks,
people shuffling from foot to foot.

Oh, I didn't realize there'd be babies.
This clerk seems to be royally pissed—
Where was your guardian angel?
Off playing what?—he's really fuming.

You're not due here for fifty-two years.
You gotta go back, get born all over again.
Here's your new passport. Go to line R.
Oh, oh—I think somebody's going to lose a halo.

Old guys' equipment is supposed to
get long and droopy—I guess
the guy behind me must be
at least a hundred and ten.

The clerk's yelling again.
I'm sick of you celebrity types;
it's a shame to waste a life on you.
You think you're entitled to special treatment?
See how you like cleaning
the Hellhound's kennels.

My turn's next. I'm very nervous.
Big smile—*Hmm, a poet and a teacher.*
You'll be in good company here.
He stamps my papers and shakes my hand.
Take the first door on the right.
Pick up your robe and wings as you go in.

Beads

I carry a string of beads wherever I go.

That very large one with the golden sheen
is Tata. It's the first one I collected.
The small silver one next to it the sister
I never met, gone before I even was.
The bright red one is my first American friend.
The swirly cobalt, the woman who made me
love my adopted language.

The warm amber one is the man who offered
to marry me if my baby's father did not.
The modest blue is a childhood chum
who could not face life after the deaths she had seen.
The one next to it is another very young friend
who never got to grow into a woman.

Those three together were Jewish—need I say more?
That bright red and purple one is someone
who browbeat me into putting words on paper
and cheered when we opened the box my books came in.
The twisty, convoluted bead is my ex-husband.

I added one just last week—a carved wooden one;
it's my sculptor friend who let her carvings say
what she could not. That one?
Let's leave the rest to talk about on another day.

Leave Taking

A door opens
unto nowhere
in an upstairs room
of a house ringed
by aged magnolias

an exit for a soul
uncertain
of its ultimate
destination

mosquito netting
hangs still as fog
muffled weeping
barely breaks
the silence

wax candles burn
their flames
do not flicker
Latin words
fall on
deaf ears

eventually
someone
shuts the door.

Christine Strevinsky was born in Poland and grew up under the Nazi occupation. She immigrated to the USA at age eighteen; she spoke no English at the time. She has been a welder, a sausage stuffer, a mail inserter, as well as being engaged in various other occupations. After raising a family she became a freshman at the age of forty-five at the University of New Orleans where she ultimately obtained a master's degree in English. She taught composition and creative writing at the Delgado Community College, also in New Orleans. She is the author of two novels, a chapbook, and has had poetry published in various literary journals (*Louisiana Journal of College English, The Magnolia Revue, Voices in the Library, The Voice of the Forum, U.S 1 Worksheets, The Magnolia Quarterly* and others), and had poems included in a couple of anthologies. She is retired and still writing. An octogenarian, she is the mother of three, grandmother of four, and a great-grandmother of three.

www.ingramcontent.com/pod-product-compliance
Lightning Source LLC
LaVergne TN
LVHW021123080426
835510LV00021B/3291